The Night Sky

A *FROZEN* DISCOVERY BOOK

By Paul Dichter

Dr. Jessie Christiansen, Consultant

Lerner Publications • Minneapolis

Lerner Publications Company
A division of Lerner Publishing Group, Inc.
241 First Avenue North
Minneapolis, MN 55401 USA

For reading levels and more information, look up this title at www.lernerbooks.com.

Main body text set in Mikado Regular 12/20.
Typeface provided by HVD Fonts.

Library of Congress Cataloging-in-Publication Data

The Cataloging-in-Publication Data for *The Night Sky: A Frozen Discovery Book* is on file at the Library of Congress.
ISBN 978-1-5415-3260-1 (lib. bdg.)
ISBN 978-1-5415-3268-7 (pbk.)
ISBN 978-1-5415-3262-5 (eb pdf)

Manufactured in the United States of America
1-44850-35720-1/16/2018

CONTENTS

WONDERS IN THE SKY

Have you ever been curious about the amazing things we see in the night sky? Olaf and his friends have! Let's explore the wonders of the night sky together!

Day and Night

Do you know why day turns into night? It's because our **planet** is always spinning. Earth makes one full spin on its axis every twenty-four hours. The side facing the **sun** experiences day. The side facing away from the sun experiences night.

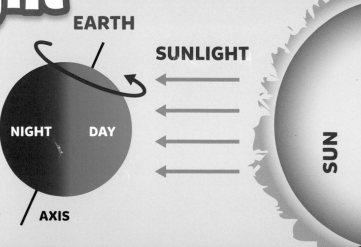

EARTH

SUNLIGHT

NIGHT · DAY

AXIS

SUN

Celestial Bodies

Celestial bodies are objects in space that we can see in our sky. The sun, **moon**, and **stars** are all celestial bodies. Which celestial bodies have you seen during the day? Which have you seen at night? Are there any that you've seen during the day *and* night?

The Day Sky

The sun is the closest star to Earth. During the day, the sun's light is so bright that we can't see any other stars. But we often see the sun shining in a blue sky.

The Night Sky

At night, we can see more celestial bodies than we can during the day. We can often see the moon and stars. Sometimes we might see planets like Venus and Jupiter.

THE NORTHERN LIGHTS

When Anna was very young, she'd tell Elsa, "The sky's awake, so I'm awake, so we have to play!" What do you think Anna meant? Let's find out!

The Aurora

What makes the sky look awake to Anna? The beautiful colors that light up the dark! What's going on? Something amazing called the **aurora**. The aurora can have many colors and shapes. Sometimes it is hard to see. Other times the whole sky is bright.

Aurora Borealis

The aurora seen from northern parts of Earth is called the **northern lights**. Usually the farther north you go, the better your chances of seeing these colorful lights. Scientists have a special name for the northern lights. They call them the **aurora borealis**.

NORTH POLE

EQUATOR

SOUTH POLE

Anna and Elsa play in the castle. Outside, lights dance in the night sky. Arendelle is a magical place!

WHAT CAUSES THE NORTHERN LIGHTS?

When Anna and Elsa were children, their parents took them on a trip. They went to the top of a tall mountain to watch the northern lights. Elsa used her magical powers to make a staircase out of snow. The sisters felt as if they were running into the colorful sky.

Solar Energy

But what causes the colorful northern lights? The answer starts with the sun. The sun is a star that is full of energy. That energy travels to Earth and gives us light and heat. Some of the sun's energy is made up of tiny specks called **electrons**.

Atmospheric
Gases

Earth is covered in an **atmosphere**. The atmosphere is a **thin** layer of **gases** including nitrogen and oxygen. These gases are the **air that we** breathe. There's no **air in** outer space. Earth's atmosphere keeps us alive!

OUTER SPACE

EARTH'S ATMOSPHERE

(nitrogen, oxygen, and other gases)

Sparks!
Flashes!

The electrons from the sun hit the gases in our atmosphere. Sometimes when they hit each other, the crash makes a spark. This spark can be a flash of color. If there are a lot of these crashes when the sky is dark and clear, we can see them. Can you guess what they are called? That's right: the aurora!

EXPLORING THE AURORA

You never forget the first time you see the northern lights. Olaf saw them on the night Elsa made him with her magic! The sky filled with wiggling, glowing green lights. What a sight!

All the Different Colors

The aurora comes in different colors. It depends on which gas from the atmosphere hits the sun's electrons. Crashes with **oxygen** are usually green. These are the most common. Sometimes they can also be red. Crashes with **nitrogen** are mostly blue. The colors can blend together too. That's why you can sometimes see purple, white, and even pink lights.

RAYS

BANDS

CORONA

All the Different Shapes

The aurora can also appear in different shapes. They ripple, pulse, glow, and make trails. They can look like curtains. They can look like blobs. They can look like waves. Scientists give the different shapes names, like rays, bands, and corona. Why are they so different from each other? Scientists aren't totally sure. It may have to do with how the electrons crash into the gases in the atmosphere. One thing we do know: they look amazing!

TROLLS, CRYSTALS, AND OTHER STORIES

Many cultures have created stories to explain the northern lights. Olaf is curious about these stories. Are you? Let's learn about some of these stories together!

Kristoff knows about the troll crystals of Arendelle. They give off a special glow. Sometimes the crystals start to go dark. Then they have to be recharged before the northern lights lose their color!

Fox Fire

The people of Finland have a story about the northern lights. They say the lights come from a fox made of fire. The fox runs on the snow into the Far North. When the fox sweeps its tail, sparks fly up into the sky. That's why they call the northern lights "fox fire."

The Valkyries

There are myths from Norway about female spirits called Valkyries. These warrior maidens watched over soldiers in battle. Some people believed the northern lights were reflections off the armor and shields of the Valkyries.

Herring Flash

In ancient Sweden, the aurora was called "herring flash." A herring is a tiny fish with bright scales. People believed the aurora was the light bouncing off these fish swimming in the sea. Seeing the herring flash meant they were about to catch a lot of fish.

SCIENCE IN ARENDELLE

In Elsa's time, people were beginning to understand the northern lights. It has taken us a long time to learn the facts. And there is still a lot more to learn! Let's find out what scientists used to think about the northern lights.

Magnetic Fields

Scientists have known for many years that Earth is a giant **magnet**. Earth's **magnetic field** affects the energy all around us. Scientists realized early on that this magnetic field had something to do with the northern lights. And they were right! The power of the magnet at the poles draws electrons from the sun.

Looking for Patterns

Scientists spend a lot of time looking and listening and measuring. They studied the northern lights for many years. They were looking for patterns. When something happens over and over, it helps us learn about it. The northern lights are hard to study. They are very unpredictable.

A telescope from Anna and Elsa's time

A Closer Look

Scientists use **telescopes** to get a closer look at objects in the sky. Telescopes are tools that make distant objects appear bigger and clearer. In the last two hundred years, telescopes have gotten much more powerful. Today we even have telescopes in space! These telescopes produce images that would have amazed scientists in Anna and Elsa's time.

Hubble Space Telescope

WHERE CAN I SEE THE LIGHTS?

Anna, Elsa, and Olaf have special memories of the northern lights. So do Kristoff and Sven! The question is, Where can you go to see these beautiful lights?

Show Me the Lights!

Where exactly can we see the northern lights on Earth? Northern countries like Sweden, Norway, and Finland are great places to look for them. Alaska and northern Canada often have good views too. You could also try Greenland, Iceland, or northern Russia. The closer you get to the **North Pole**, the easier they are to see.

Polar Lights

The north isn't the only place you can see the aurora. You can also see auroras in the south. Those are called the **southern lights**. The farther you get from the **equator**, the more likely you are to see auroras! The northern lights and southern lights are also called the **polar lights**.

NORTHERN LIGHTS

EQUATOR

SOUTHERN LIGHTS

Aurora Australis

The southern lights have another name. They are called the **aurora australis**. They can be seen from New Zealand, Australia, South America, and Antarctica. As with the northern lights, the closer you are to the pole, the better your view!

COLD PLACES

Arendelle is a beautiful kingdom. There is a castle and a town. There are fjords, forests, and mountains. It gets very cold there in the winter. Parts of the kingdom are tundras. What do you know about the tundra?

The Tundra

The **tundra** is a very cold region with very few trees. Winters last a long time in the tundra. Summers are short. Some tundra regions are located high in the mountains. The purple areas in this map are tundras.

People

Few people live in the Arctic. But one group of people has lived in Arctic regions for thousands of years. They are called the Sami people. They live in parts of Norway, Sweden, Finland, and Russia. Traditionally, they have made a living by fishing and by herding reindeer.

Animals

Lots of animals live in the tundra. These include owls, foxes, wolves, and reindeer. Foxes and reindeer have thick fur that protects them from the cold. Arctic wolves have fur on their paws that gives them a better grip on the icy ground. Some animals, like huskies, even help people get around! These dogs are very strong and can pull sleds for a long time.

Plants

What kinds of plants grow in the tundra? Short ones! It's so cold and windy that big plants have trouble surviving. But there are a lot of small plants like mosses and shrubs!

WHEN TO WATCH THE LIGHTS

Anna and Elsa love to watch the northern lights. So do their friends. But it's not enough for them to be in the right place. It also has to be the right time! Let's learn about the best time to watch the northern lights.

What Time of Day?

The skies have to be dark to see the northern lights. Otherwise, sunlight will block them out. In the Far North, it can get dark very early in the winter. Some people think the best time to see the aurora is between 9:30 p.m. and 1:30 a.m. That's pretty late!

What Time of Year?

Winter is the best time to see the northern lights. Why is that? Because the sun sets earlier and rises later. In some northern regions, you can see the aurora as early as 4 p.m.! Winter nights in the north are long and dark. This makes it easier to see the northern lights.

The Solar Cycle

Our sun has a magnetic field, just like Earth. Every eleven years, the sun's magnetic activity is very high. This is called the **solar maximum**. This is the best time to see the auroras because it's when the sun's energy is the strongest. The auroras are very active for two years before and two years after the solar maximum.

WHAT CAUSES THE SEASONS?

Do you know what Olaf's favorite season is? It's summer! Do you know why we have different seasons? Keep reading to find out!

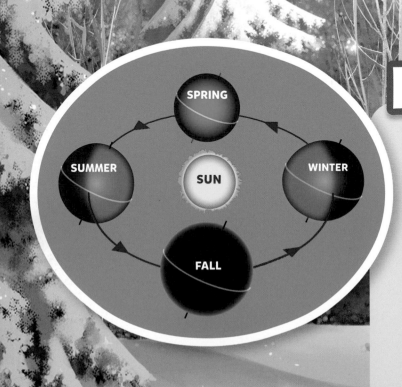

SPRING

SUMMER

SUN

WINTER

FALL

Earth's Tilt

We experience different seasons because Earth is tilted. The tilt of the Earth changes how much sunlight gets to different parts of Earth. When the northern part of Earth is close to the sun, it's warmer there. That is summer. When the sun is farther from the northern part of Earth, it's colder there. That is winter. In between, we have fall and spring.

Hemispheres and Seasons

Winter does not happen at the same time all over the world. The bottom half of Earth has opposite seasons from the top half. When it's summer in the **Northern Hemisphere**, it's winter in the **Southern Hemisphere**.

NORTHERN HEMISPHERE (summer)

SUNLIGHT

SOUTHERN HEMISPHERE (winter)

SPRING

SUMMER

FALL

WINTER

Seasonal Weather

Have you noticed changes in the weather as seasons change? Maybe it's cold and snowy in winter but warm and rainy in spring. Summer might be hot and sunny, while fall is cool and windy. These changes are related to Earth's tilt and the path our planet travels around the sun.

Dressing for the Weather

When it's cold out, it's very important to stay warm! A good way to do this is to cover as much skin as you can. Wearing a jacket, gloves, scarf, and hat will help. Anna found warm clothes at Oaken's Trading Post when Elsa created a snowstorm during summer. Can you point out all the items that help her stay warm?

DAYLIGHT AND NIGHTFALL

Anna, Elsa, and their friends love to go on adventures! Not all their adventures happen during the day. Sometimes they find themselves out at night. How much do you know about night and day?

Midnight Sun

The farther north or south you get, the more Earth's tilt matters. In the Far North, the sun is so high in the sky during summer that it doesn't always fully set. This is called the **midnight sun**. The same is true in the Far South.

Polar Night

In the winter, the opposite is true! The sun is so low that it's dark for long stretches of time. This is called **polar night**. Around the equator, the sun is always high in the sky. It stays fairly warm year-round. And the time of sunrises and sunsets doesn't change much.

Solstices and Equinoxes

In many countries, the **summer solstice** is the first day of summer. It's the longest day of the year! The **winter solstice** is the shortest day of the year. It marks the first day of winter in many places. The days and nights are of similar lengths during the fall and spring. It's called an **equinox** when day and night are exactly the same length. There are two of those—one in the fall and one in the spring.

EQUINOX (March)

SOLSTICE (June)

SUN

SOLSTICE (December)

EQUINOX (September)

LATE-NIGHT STARGAZING

Looking at the night sky can be really fun! Kristoff sings a song for Olaf, Anna, Elsa, and Sven. The friends enjoy the music as the northern lights dance above.

When the Sun Goes Down

You can't see the stars until the sun sets. The sun goes down at different times throughout the year. In the summer, you might have to stay up late to see the sun go down. The sun sets very early in winter, especially in the Far North.

What to Bring

You might want to bring a few things with you when you go **stargazing**. Make sure you dress warmly! If you're going to lie down on the ground, you might like a blanket to lie on. Binoculars can help you see things in the night sky. Another helpful tool is a flashlight covered with red cellophane. This will help you see in the dark without ruining your night vision.

Get Some Sleep!

As fun as it is to stargaze, it's also really important to get a good night's sleep. Kids need about ten hours of sleep every night. If you do stay up after dark to look at the stars, make sure you can sleep late the next day. Sleep is important. Just ask Kristoff!

THE STARS IN THE SKY

On a clear night, we can see thousands of stars in the sky. During the day, we can see only one: our sun! Olaf loves feeling the warmth of the sun's rays. Let's learn more about our sun and other stars.

What Are Stars?

What exactly are stars? They're giant spheres of hot gas. They create huge amounts of energy. They're like power plants! We experience our sun's energy as light and heat. Stars can live for billions of years. They are different sizes and even different colors. The coolest stars are red. The hottest stars are white or blue. Even the coolest star is very hot.

Our Sun

Our sun is the closest star to Earth. Earth **orbits** around the sun. It takes a year for Earth to travel around the sun one time. Here are some sun facts that may amaze you. The sun is 93 million miles (150 million km) away from us. It is 4.5 billion years old. The center of the sun is 27 million degrees Fahrenheit (15 million degrees C). Wow, that's hot!

Galaxies

Giant groups of stars are called **galaxies**. Stars usually spin around the center of their galaxy, just as Earth spins around the sun. Many galaxies are shaped like spirals.

The Milky Way

We are in a spiral galaxy called the **Milky Way**. There are at least one hundred billion stars in the Milky Way. It takes our sun more than two hundred million years to orbit around the center of the galaxy. What we can see of our galaxy from Earth looks like a milky band across the sky. That's why ancient people called it the Milky Way.

NAVIGATING BY THE STARS

Arendelle has a strong tradition of sailing. Maps and compasses can help people sail from one place to another. But did you know that stars can also help sailors navigate? Let's find out how!

The North Star

Many sailors use the **North Star** to help them navigate. **Navigation** means figuring out where you are and where you want to go. The North Star is a bright star seen in the Northern Hemisphere. Its scientific name is **Polaris**. The stars "move" in the sky as Earth rotates, but the North Star stays in the same place. This photo was taken over many hours. Can you find the North Star?

Constellations

A **constellation** is a group of stars that form a shape in the sky. Throughout history, travelers have used constellations to help them navigate. Many constellations are named after animals. Some are named after people or mythical creatures. Have you heard of the **Big Dipper**? It is part of a constellation called Ursa Major, or "Great Bear." The two stars at the end of the dipper point directly at the North Star. The North Star is part of the constellation called the Little Dipper.

LITTLE DIPPER

POLARIS (NORTH STAR)

BIG DIPPER

The Southern Cross

SOUTHERN CROSS

points toward the SOUTH CELESTIAL POLE

The North Star can be seen only in the Northern Hemisphere. What if you are south of that? In the Southern Hemisphere, travelers use a constellation called the **Southern Cross** to help them navigate. The long bar of the cross points to the **south celestial pole**. This is the point in the sky directly above the **South Pole**.

DISCOVERING THE PLANETS

Where does Olaf live? Arendelle! Olaf loves learning everything about his home. How well do you know your town? Your country? Your planet?

SATURN

NEPTUNE

Planets

What are planets? We're on one right now! Planets are large bodies that orbit around a star. Our planet, Earth, orbits around the sun. Some planets, like Earth, are made of rock and dirt. Other planets are made of gas. Saturn is one example. Planets such as Neptune are made of both gas and ice.

The Solar System

All the planets that orbit our sun are part of the **solar system**. There are eight planets plus some dwarf planets. The closest planet to the sun is Mercury. Mercury travels around the sun in only eighty-eight days. The farthest planet is Neptune. It takes Neptune 165 years to travel around the sun! Pluto is one of the dwarf planets. It's too small to be a full planet. It's even farther away from the sun than Neptune!

SUN

MERCURY | EARTH | JUPITER | URANUS | PLUTO
VENUS | MARS | SATURN | NEPTUNE

The Planet We Call Home

Earth is the third planet from the sun. We think it's the only planet in the solar system that can support life. The other planets don't have air that we can breathe. They are also either too hot or too cold.

THE MOON

When Anna met Prince Hans, she thought she had found true love. Hans turned out to be a villain. But Anna still remembers how bright and beautiful the moon was that night.

Meet Our Moon

A moon is an object that orbits a planet. Some planets have many moons. Our planet has one. Our moon orbits Earth about every twenty-seven days. Have you noticed that the moon changes shape? Sometimes it looks like a circle in the sky. Sometimes it's half a circle. Sometimes we can't see it at all! What is going on? It has to do with where the moon is when the sun shines on it.

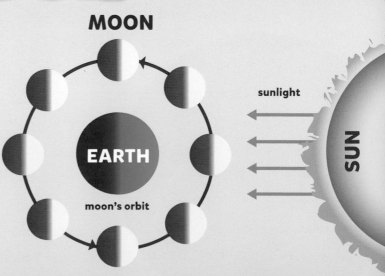

MOON

sunlight

EARTH

SUN

moon's orbit

Phases of the Moon

The different shapes of the moon we see are called **phases**. When Earth is between the moon and the sun, we can see a full moon. When the moon is between the sun and Earth, it's invisible. This is called a new moon. In between these phases, it can be a crescent moon, a gibbous moon, or a quarter moon. So many phases!

| NEW MOON | CRESCENT MOON | QUARTER MOON | GIBBOUS MOON | FULL MOON | GIBBOUS MOON | QUARTER MOON | CRESCENT MOON |

The Far Side of the Moon

Did you know that the same side of the moon always faces Earth? This is because the moon turns at just the right speed as it orbits Earth. Have you heard the expression "the dark side of the moon"? There actually isn't a dark side of the moon. All parts of the moon get sunlight. We just can't see the far side from Earth.

ECLIPSES

What follows you around everywhere you go? Your shadow! Shadows are made when light can't shine through something. People have shadows. Objects have shadows. Even snowmen have shadows. Just look at Olaf!

What Is an Eclipse?

Earth and the moon have shadows too. What happens when an object in space moves into the shadow of another object? An **eclipse**. On Earth, there are two kinds of eclipses. They both involve the sun and the moon. Let's learn about them!

Solar Eclipse

Solar eclipses happen when the moon gets between Earth and the sun. They occur once every eighteen months. A total solar eclipse happens when the sun, the moon, and Earth are in a straight line. If you're in the right place, the sun will go dark—and so will the sky! Solar eclipses last only for a few minutes. Never look right at a solar eclipse. It can harm your eyes.

area of total eclipse

SUN   MOON   EARTH

Lunar Eclipse

A **lunar eclipse** happens when Earth gets between the sun and the moon. The moon is in Earth's shadow. We can still see the moon during a total lunar eclipse. Why is that? Because some light gets bent by Earth's atmosphere and hits the moon. The moon looks red during a lunar eclipse.

SUN   EARTH   MOON

COMETS AND METEORS

Anna loves to look at the night sky. There are so many wondrous things to see. There are stars, planets, the moon, and even the northern lights! Anna never gets tired of looking up. Is that a shooting star? Let's find out.

Comets

There's a lot more to space than planets, stars, and moons. Do you know about **comets**? Comets are big balls made mostly of ice. They are too small to be planets. They orbit around stars and have tails that we can see in the sky. The tails are made from the ice heated by the sun and turned into a gas.

Meteoroids, Meteors, and Meteorites

Meteoroids are rocks in space. Sometimes these rocks hit Earth. As they travel through our atmosphere, they often burn up and turn into dust. When they burn, we can see a streak of light. This is called a **meteor**. Sometimes the rock doesn't completely burn up. Some of it makes it to the ground. The part that lands is called a **meteorite**.

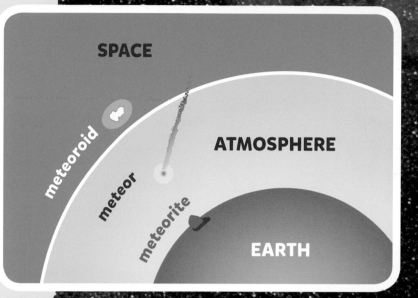

SPACE

meteoroid

ATMOSPHERE

meteor

meteorite

EARTH

What Are Shooting Stars?

Have you ever seen a shooting star? Did you know that shooting stars aren't actually stars at all? They're meteors! Thousands of meteors streak through Earth's sky every day. Sometimes Earth passes through an area where a comet once traveled. Comets can leave a trail of dust behind them. When Earth moves through this trail, it can create a **meteor shower**. This is when we can see lots of meteors in a single night.

BEST VIEWING CONDITIONS

Anna and Elsa are lucky. Arendelle is a great place to look at the night sky! The stars shine bright, and the northern lights glow. Let's learn about the best conditions for seeing things in the night sky.

Cloudy or Clear?

Sometimes it can be cloudy at night. Clouds can make it hard to see the stars and even the moon. The best time to go stargazing is on a clear night. Then you might even see a meteor or two!

Light Pollution

A dark sky is just as important as a clear sky. The darker it is, the more you can see! If you live in a city, you might have to deal with **light pollution**. Light pollution means that the lights on Earth are so bright that they block out the light of the stars. A full moon can also add to light pollution. The light from the full moon is so bright that it can make it hard to see many stars.

Outside the City

If you can get away from the glow of city lights, you can see so much more in the night sky. In a city, you might be able to see only ten stars. On a clear night far from city lights, you can see about twenty-five hundred stars in the sky! The longer you look, the more your eyes get used to the dark. This means you can see even more stars.

GOODBYE FOR NOW!

With the help of Anna, Elsa, Olaf, Kristoff, and Sven, we've learned so much about the night sky! We've learned about the northern lights. We've learned about stars and planets. We've learned about our sun and our moon. We've learned about comets and meteors. And we've learned about when and where to see some of the wonderful sights in the night sky.

Now it's your turn to take what you know and go look at the night sky. Plan a stargazing night with family and friends. Sharing the beauty of the night sky can be a magical experience!

GLOSSARY

atmosphere: a thin layer of gases around a planet or star

aurora: the scientific name for the polar lights

aurora australis: the scientific name for the southern lights

aurora borealis: the scientific name for the northern lights

Big Dipper: a group of stars shaped like a spoon or ladle. It is part of the Ursa Major constellation.

celestial body: an object in space

comet: a big ball of ice that orbits around a star and has a tail of gas and dust

constellation: a group of stars that form a shape in the sky

eclipse: when an object in space moves into the shadow of another object

electron: a tiny speck of energy with a negative charge

equator: a line exactly halfway between the North Pole and the South Pole that circles Earth

equinox: a day when day and night are of equal length

galaxy: a very large group of stars

gas: a substance, such as air, that has no shape

light pollution: when lights on Earth are so bright that they make it hard to see stars in the night sky

lunar eclipse: an event that happens when Earth gets between the sun and the moon

magnet: an object that can pull similar objects toward itself

magnetic field: the area around a magnet where you can feel the magnetic force

meteor: a meteoroid that burns and glows in Earth's atmosphere

meteorite: a meteoroid that lands on Earth's surface

meteoroid: a rock in space

meteor shower: a large group of meteors caused by Earth passing through an area with a lot of rocks and dust

midnight sun: when the sun is so high near the North Pole or South Pole that it is visible even at midnight

Milky Way: the galaxy that Earth is in

moon: a natural object that orbits a planet

navigation: figuring out where you are and where you want to go

nitrogen: a gas that makes up most of Earth's atmosphere

Northern Hemisphere: the top half of Earth

northern lights: glowing lights that can be seen in northern night skies

North Pole: the most northern point on Earth

North Star: the star in the Northern Hemisphere that shows where the north celestial pole is. It is also called Polaris.

orbit: to move around an object in a circular path

oxygen: a gas in air that we need to breathe in order to live

phase: a shape of the sunlit part of the moon as seen from Earth

planet: a body in space that travels around a star and is shaped like a sphere

Polaris: the scientific name for the North Star

polar lights: the northern lights and the southern lights. It is another name for auroras.

polar night: when the sun is so low near the North Pole or South Pole that it doesn't rise for more than twenty-four hours

solar eclipse: an event that happens when the moon gets between Earth and the sun

solar maximum: the time every eleven years when the sun's magnetic activity is the greatest

solar system: the sun and the planets, moons, and other objects that orbit around it

south celestial pole: a point in the sky directly above the South Pole

South Pole: the most southern point on Earth

Southern Cross: a constellation in the Southern Hemisphere that points to the south celestial pole

Southern Hemisphere: the bottom half of Earth

southern lights: glowing lights that can be seen in southern night skies

star: an object in space that shines with its own light and energy

stargazing: looking up at the stars

summer solstice: the longest day of the year. It is also the first day of summer in many countries.

sun: the star around which our planet spins

telescope: a device you look through that makes distant objects appear bigger and clearer

tundra: parts of the world that have no trees and are very cold

winter solstice: the shortest day of the year. It is also the first day of winter in many countries.

INDEX

PHOTO CREDITS